A Deep Dive into Large Language Models: Exploring

the Power of Bloom, Vicuna, PaLM, Cohere, Falcon

40B, and Beyond

Contents

Part I: Introduction to Large Language Models (LLMs)

Chapter 1: What are LLMs?

Definition and core concepts:

- Large language models (LLMs) are a type of artificial intelligence (AI) that excel at processing and understanding human language.

- Imagine them as incredibly powerful computer programs that have been trained on massive amounts of text data, allowing them to perform tasks like generating text, translating languages, writing different kinds of creative content, and answering your questions in an informative way.

- At their core, LLMs rely on a technique called **deep learning**, which involves training complex algorithms on vast amounts of data. This data can include books, articles, code, and even conversations, allowing the LLM to learn the patterns and rules of language.

Applications of LLMs:

- LLMs have a wide range of applications that are constantly evolving. Some examples include:

    o **Generating creative text formats:** They can write different kinds of creative content, like poems, code, scripts, musical pieces, and even email.

- Machine translation: LLMs can translate languages more accurately and naturally than ever before.
- Chatbots and virtual assistants: They can power chatbots and virtual assistants that can have more engaging and informative conversations with users.
- Summarization and question answering: LLMs can condense large amounts of text into summaries and answer your questions in an informative way, even if they are open ended or challenging.
- Text generation and completion: They can be used to complete sentences, come

up with creative text formats, and even write different kinds of creative content.

Benefits and limitations of LLMs:

- **Benefits:** LLMs offer significant advantages, such as:

  - **Automation of tasks:** They can automate tasks that previously required human intervention, such as content creation, translation, and data analysis.

  - **Improved efficiency:** LLMs can process information and complete tasks much faster than humans.

  - **Enhanced creativity:** They can assist with creative tasks and generate new ideas.

- **Accessibility:** LLMs can help break down language barriers and make information more accessible to everyone.

- **Limitations:** It's important to be aware of LLM limitations as well:

  - **Bias:** LLMs can inherit biases from the data they are trained on.

  - **Limited understanding:** While they can process language well, they may not always understand the true meaning or context of what they are communicating.

  - **Factual inaccuracies:** Sometimes, LLMs can generate text that is factually incorrect or misleading.

- **Ethical considerations:** The development and use of LLMs raise important ethical questions that need to be addressed.

Chapter 2: Understanding LLM Training and Architecture

Training data and pre-training:

- The secret sauce behind LLMs lies in the massive amount of data they are trained on. This data can include text from books, articles, code, websites, and even social media.

- A crucial step in LLM training is called **pre-training**. In this phase, the LLM is not given a specific task, but rather learns the general patterns and relationships between words in the vast amount of data. This pre-training equips the LLM with a strong foundation for tackling specific tasks later.

Transformer architecture and its role in LLMs:

- A key piece of technology that powers LLMs is the **transformer architecture**. This is a specific type of neural network that excels at analyzing sequential data, like text.

- Transformers can analyze the relationships between words in a sentence, allowing the LLM to understand the context and meaning of the language it's processing.

Fine-tuning for specific tasks:

- Once an LLM has been pre-trained, it can be **fine-tuned** for specific tasks. This involves training the LLM on a smaller dataset that is specific to the desired task.

- For example, if you want an LLM to be a good translator, you would fine-tune it on a dataset of translated texts. Fine-tuning allows the LLM to leverage its pre-trained knowledge and apply it to solve a particular problem.

Chapter 2: Understanding LLM Training and Architecture

This chapter dives into the inner workings of LLMs, exploring how they learn and what makes them tick. We'll break down three key concepts: training data and pre-training, the transformer architecture, and fine-tuning for specific tasks.

Training data and pre-training:

Imagine a child learning a language. They're exposed to a vast amount of spoken and written words, absorbing the basic building blocks and how they fit together. Similarly, LLMs are trained on massive amounts of text data. This data can be a digital library containing books, articles, code, and even social media conversations. The more data an LLM is exposed to, the richer its understanding of language becomes.

However, there's a crucial step before throwing all this data at an LLM: **pre-training**. Here's the analogy: before a child can write a story, they need to grasp the alphabet, grammar, and basic sentence structure. Pre-training works similarly. Instead of giving the LLM a specific task, it's presented with the vast amount of text data. The LLM's job is to analyze this data and learn the fundamental patterns and relationships between words. It essentially builds a strong foundation in language – understanding how words connect, how sentences are formed, and the statistical likelihood of one word following another.

Think of pre-training as teaching the LLM the "rules" of language. This pre-trained model becomes the base upon which further learning can happen.

Transformer architecture and its role in LLMs:

The transformer architecture is like the brain of an LLM. It's a specific type of artificial neural network designed to excel at analyzing sequential data –

perfect for handling language, which relies on the order of words. Here's what makes transformers special:

- **Attention mechanism:** Unlike traditional neural networks that process information sequentially, transformers can pay attention to all parts of a sentence simultaneously. Imagine reading a sentence – a transformer can not only understand each word but also how each word relates to the others, giving it a deeper grasp of context and meaning.
- **Parallel processing:** Transformers can analyze different parts of a sentence at once, making

them much faster and more efficient than traditional models.

Think of the transformer as a powerful tool that allows the LLM to not only understand individual words but also how they interact within a sentence, giving it a more nuanced understanding of language.

Fine-tuning for specific tasks:

After pre-training, the LLM has a solid foundation in language. But now, it's time to get specific! This is where **fine-tuning** comes in. Imagine a pre-trained LLM as a talented musician who can play many instruments. Fine-tuning is like giving them a specific musical piece to learn.

For a particular task, the LLM is exposed to a smaller, more focused dataset. For example, if we want the LLM to become a translation expert, we'd fine-tune it on a dataset of translated texts from various languages. This allows the LLM to leverage its pre-trained knowledge of language and apply it to this specific domain. The fine-tuning process helps the LLM become proficient in a particular task, making it a true language whiz in that area.

Part II: Deep Dive into Specific LLM Technologies

This section delves into the details of some prominent LLM technologies, exploring their unique characteristics and capabilities.

Chapter 3: Bloom (Google AI)

- **Technical Specifications:** Bloom is a colossal LLM from Google AI, boasting a massive parameter count (often indicative of an LLM's capabilities). While the exact number remains undisclosed, it's known to be in the hundreds of billions, making it one of the largest LLMs in existence. Bloom is likely trained on a diverse dataset of text and code, allowing it to perform various tasks.

- **Strengths:** Bloom excels at tasks requiring a broad understanding of language. Its massive size allows it to handle complex reasoning and generate creative text formats like poems or code. Additionally, Bloom might be adept at tasks involving factual language understanding due to its extensive training data.

- **Weaknesses:** Due to its immense size, Bloom might be computationally expensive to run. Additionally, the vastness of its training data could introduce biases if not carefully curated. There's also the possibility of Bloom generating factually incorrect outputs, especially for very specific or technical information.

- **Use Cases and Applications:** Bloom's strengths make it suitable for tasks like writing different kinds of creative content, generating different creative text formats, and answering open ended, challenging, or strange questions. It might also be useful for summarizing complex information or for code generation.

Chapter 4: Vicuna (Meta AI)

- **Technical Specifications:** Vicuna is a large LLM developed by Meta AI. Vicuna likely utilizes the transformer architecture for its core functionality.

- **Strengths:** Multilinguality is Vicuna's key strength. It can translate languages effectively, understand text in various languages, and potentially even generate creative text formats in different languages.

- **Weaknesses:** Since details are scarce, it's difficult to pinpoint specific weaknesses. However, Vicuna might not be as adept at tasks requiring a deep understanding of a specific domain or culture compared to LLMs trained on focused datasets.

- **Use Cases and Applications:** Vicuna's multilingual capabilities make it a prime candidate for machine translation tasks. It could also be used for tasks requiring understanding text in multiple languages, or potentially for generating creative text formats across different languages.

Chapter 5: PaLM (Google AI)

- **Technical Specifications:** PaLM (Pathway Language Model) is another heavyweight LLM from Google AI. It boasts a massive parameter count and is trained on a pathway system, allowing it to access and process information from different modalities beyond just text.

- **Strengths:** PaLM's pathway system grants it the ability to not only understand text but also potentially leverage information from images, code, or other formats. This makes it a powerful tool for tasks requiring a multimodal understanding of the world. Additionally, its massive size likely grants it strong capabilities in general language processing tasks.

- **Weaknesses:** Similar to Bloom, PaLM's immense size might make it computationally expensive. Additionally, the complexity of its training data could introduce challenges in interpretability and potential for bias.

- **Use Cases and Applications:** PaLM's multimodal capabilities make it suitable for tasks that require understanding information from various sources. It could be used for tasks like question answering that involve not just text but also images or other data formats. Additionally, its strength in general language processing makes it applicable to a wide range of text-based tasks.

Chapter 6: Cohere

- **Technical Overview:** Due to the proprietary nature of Cohere technology, specifics about their models are not publicly available. However, we can discuss LLMs in general.

- **Strengths:** Based on available information, Cohere models are known for their focus on specific tasks and domains. This allows them to achieve high accuracy in those areas. Additionally, Cohere emphasizes interpretability and explainability of their models, making them more trustworthy and easier to debug.

- **Weaknesses:** Since Cohere models are focused on specific tasks, they might not be as versatile as some other LLMs for general language processing tasks. Additionally, limited information about their inner workings makes it difficult to assess potential biases or limitations.

- **Use Cases and Applications:** Cohere models are likely well-suited for tasks requiring high accuracy in specific domains, like legal

document analysis, medical report processing,

or e-commerce product descriptions.

Chapter 7: Falcon

Technical Specifications: Falcon 40B is a large LLM

developed by Tsinghua University. It boasts 40 billion

parameters, making it a substantial model. While

specifics are limited, it likely utilizes the transformer

architecture for its core functionality.

- **Strengths:** Falcon 40B is known for its efficiency

  and focus on factual language understanding.

  This makes it suitable for tasks requiring

  accurate information retrieval and analysis.

  Additionally, its large size suggests it might have

good capabilities in general language processing tasks.

- **Weaknesses:** There might be limitations in understanding complex or creative language compared to LLMs trained on broader datasets. Additionally, information about potential biases or limitations in specific domains might be limited.

- **Use Cases and Applications:** Falcon 40B's strength in factual language understanding makes it a good fit for tasks like question answering that require accurate information retrieval. It could also be useful for tasks like text summarization or information extraction from factual documents.

Exploring the Power of Bloom: Understanding Large-Scale Multilingual Model Dynamics

Bloom stands as a benchmark in the field of multilingual large language models (LLMs), pushing the boundaries of what open collaboration and cutting-edge architecture can achieve. Its significance lies not just in its sheer scale but in its ability to understand and generate coherent responses across a plethora of languages, making it a game-changer for global applications.

At its core, Bloom represents a blend of innovation and inclusivity. Trained on 176 billion parameters, it was designed with a commitment to diversity, processing data in over 46 natural and 13 programming languages. This multilingual capability emerges from a meticulously curated training dataset, sourced through collective efforts and governed by ethical guidelines. Unlike traditional monolingual LLMs, Bloom's ability to handle low-resource languages underscores its transformative potential in bridging linguistic divides.

The architecture of Bloom is an engineering marvel. Leveraging the power of transformer-based frameworks, it employs state-of-the-art techniques such as attention mechanisms and optimized layer design. These features enable Bloom to manage context over extended sequences, ensuring the coherence and relevance of its responses. Such an approach enhances Bloom's performance in tasks like document summarization, machine translation, and conversational AI.

One of the standout aspects of Bloom's development was its transparent and collaborative nature. Built under the BigScience initiative, it brought together researchers, engineers, and data scientists from around the globe. This community-driven approach not only democratized AI research but also ensured that Bloom's deployment adhered to strict ethical standards. Unlike proprietary models, Bloom's open-access nature encourages a wide range of applications, from academic research to industry-specific innovations.

Despite its achievements, Bloom is not without challenges. Its large parameter size demands significant computational resources, posing questions about accessibility and environmental impact. Moreover, while its multilingual capability is impressive, the quality of responses in low-resource languages still lags behind major languages like English and Spanish. Addressing these issues requires ongoing refinement and possibly hybrid approaches involving smaller, specialized models.

From a practical perspective, Bloom has already demonstrated its utility in diverse domains. In healthcare, it aids in translating medical documents into underserved languages, thereby improving patient care in remote regions. In education, it serves as a powerful tool for creating multilingual content, enabling access to learning materials across borders. Such applications highlight the tangible benefits of investing in multilingual AI systems.

As Bloom continues to evolve, its role in the broader AI ecosystem grows. The development of similar models inspired by its framework indicates the rising importance of multilingual LLMs in a globalized world. By addressing its limitations and building upon its strengths, Bloom sets a precedent for future endeavors in AI research and deployment.

Vicuna's Approach to Fine-Tuning: Breaking Barriers in Accessible AI

Vicuna represents a critical evolution in the world of fine-tuned LLMs, emphasizing accessibility and affordability without compromising performance. Unlike many proprietary models requiring immense computational resources, Vicuna showcases how effective and efficient fine-tuning can unlock the potential of smaller models for real-world applications.

Central to Vicuna's design is its use of the LoRA (Low-Rank Adaptation) method for fine-tuning. This technique allows for incremental updates to pre-trained LLMs without requiring the retraining of the entire model. By targeting specific parameters and layers, LoRA drastically reduces the computational overhead and memory requirements, making advanced LLM capabilities accessible even to smaller organizations and individual developers.

Vicuna's training approach focuses on domain-specific customization. Instead of relying on general-purpose training datasets, it fine-tunes pre-trained models using carefully curated datasets tailored to specific industries or use cases. This targeted approach enhances its performance in areas like legal document analysis, healthcare diagnostics, and customer service chatbots.

An essential feature of Vicuna is its adaptability to low-resource environments. By integrating sparse training techniques and model compression strategies, Vicuna can operate effectively on hardware with limited capabilities. This innovation is particularly impactful for applications in developing regions where access to high-end computational infrastructure is scarce.

The ethical considerations embedded in Vicuna's development are equally noteworthy. Its creators prioritized transparency and fairness by ensuring the training datasets were free from harmful biases. Additionally, Vicuna's open-access framework promotes collaborative research, allowing developers to experiment with and adapt the model for novel applications.

Vicuna's real-world applications demonstrate its versatility. In the legal field, it assists in summarizing complex contracts and legal briefs, saving time and resources for law firms. In healthcare, it facilitates medical coding and billing by analyzing patient records and ensuring accurate documentation. These examples underscore Vicuna's potential to revolutionize industries that rely heavily on text analysis and information retrieval.

Challenges remain, particularly in balancing fine-tuning efficiency with generalization capabilities. Over-specialization can limit Vicuna's adaptability to new tasks or domains. Future iterations may explore hybrid approaches that combine fine-tuning with continual learning, ensuring the model remains

versatile while excelling in specialized tasks.

Pioneering Large-Scale Models: A Deep Dive into Google's PaLM

Google's PaLM (Pathways Language Model) represents a paradigm shift in LLM development, showcasing unprecedented scalability and versatility. Designed as part of Google's Pathways initiative, PaLM leverages a unified architecture to perform a diverse array of tasks, setting new benchmarks in both general-purpose and domain-specific AI applications.

PaLM's architecture is a testament to engineering excellence. With over 540 billion parameters, it employs sparse activation techniques to optimize resource usage without compromising performance. This sparse activation ensures that only relevant sections of the model are engaged during inference, reducing computational costs and enhancing efficiency.

Training PaLM involved the use of Google's TPU v4 infrastructure, enabling distributed training across thousands of accelerators. This setup allowed PaLM to process enormous amounts of data within a reasonable timeframe, demonstrating the power of cutting-edge hardware in scaling AI models.

One of PaLM's defining features is its ability to perform few-shot and zero-shot learning with remarkable accuracy. By leveraging its vast training data and sophisticated architecture, PaLM can generalize knowledge to new tasks with minimal additional training. This capability is particularly valuable in applications like conversational AI, where the model must adapt to diverse user queries and contexts.

PaLM's contributions to ethical AI are also significant. Google implemented rigorous auditing processes during its development, ensuring the model adhered to strict guidelines for fairness, transparency, and privacy. These measures included dataset scrutiny to eliminate biases and the integration of safeguards to prevent misuse.

Real-world applications of PaLM highlight its transformative potential. In scientific research, it aids in complex data analysis, such as protein folding simulations and climate modeling. In the creative arts, it generates high-quality textual and visual content, enabling new forms of storytelling and artistic expression. Such use cases exemplify the multifaceted capabilities of LLMs in driving innovation across domains.

Harnessing Falcon 40B for Enterprise-Grade Applications

Falcon 40B emerges as a robust solution for enterprises seeking scalable and efficient AI solutions tailored to business needs. Designed with a focus on practicality, Falcon 40B bridges the gap between cutting-edge research and real-world deployment, making it a preferred choice for organizations aiming to integrate AI into their operations.

The model's architecture reflects a balance between performance and resource efficiency. While leveraging advanced techniques like attention optimization and parameter sharing, Falcon 40B maintains a manageable size that facilitates deployment on standard enterprise hardware. This design philosophy aligns with the growing demand for scalable AI solutions that do not require excessive computational resources.

Training Falcon 40B involved a mix of proprietary and public datasets, ensuring a diverse knowledge base while prioritizing data security and compliance. This approach enhances the model's utility in industries with strict regulatory requirements, such as finance and healthcare.

Falcon 40B excels in tasks that require high accuracy and consistency. Its deployment in customer service automation has demonstrated significant improvements in response time and customer satisfaction. Similarly, its application in financial analysis enables real-time insights, aiding decision-making processes in trading and investment.

Challenges in Falcon 40B's adoption include the need for customization to specific industries and tasks. To address this, developers have introduced modular training techniques, allowing enterprises to fine-tune the model for their unique requirements without

extensive retraining.

Cohere's Generative AI: Shaping Conversational Intelligence

Cohere's approach to generative AI emphasizes simplicity and accessibility, offering tools that empower developers to build sophisticated conversational systems with minimal technical barriers. Unlike monolithic LLMs, Cohere's solutions are designed for seamless integration into existing workflows, catering to a wide range of use cases.

The core strength of Cohere lies in its modular architecture. By offering APIs that encapsulate complex language understanding and generation capabilities, Cohere simplifies the deployment of AI systems. This modularity enables businesses to integrate advanced language features into their applications without requiring deep expertise in AI.

Cohere's training methodologies prioritize efficiency and inclusivity. The use of smaller, specialized models trained on domain-specific data ensures high performance while reducing resource demands. This strategy aligns with the company's mission to democratize access to AI, making it feasible for small and medium-sized enterprises to adopt advanced technologies.

In practical terms, Cohere's solutions have been widely adopted in areas like customer support, content creation, and market analysis. For example, its integration into e-commerce platforms enables personalized recommendations and dynamic content generation, enhancing the shopping experience.

While Cohere has made significant strides in accessibility, challenges remain in ensuring the robustness and fairness of its models. Addressing these concerns requires ongoing efforts in data validation and the development of tools for monitoring and mitigating biases in AI systems.

Advanced Adaptation: Customizing Falcon 40B for Specialized Industries

Falcon 40B's modularity and scalability allow it to be fine-tuned for specific industries, unlocking its potential in domains that require precision, compliance, and contextual understanding. This adaptability stems from its core design, which supports efficient customization while maintaining general-purpose capabilities.

In the healthcare industry, Falcon 40B has demonstrated remarkable proficiency in processing electronic health records (EHRs), automating medical coding, and generating summaries for complex clinical documentation. Fine-tuning for this domain involves integrating domain-specific datasets, such as medical terminologies and diagnostic codes, to enhance the model's accuracy and relevance.

In finance, Falcon 40B is employed for sentiment analysis, fraud detection, and risk assessment. Customizing the model for these applications requires training on financial news, transaction data, and regulatory documents. Its ability to parse vast datasets and identify patterns enables institutions to make data-driven decisions with speed and confidence.

The legal industry benefits from Falcon 40B's capability to analyze contracts, legal briefs, and case law. By leveraging advanced tokenization and context retention, the model can summarize lengthy documents and identify critical clauses or discrepancies, saving significant time for legal professionals.

Despite its adaptability, fine-tuning Falcon 40B for specific domains poses challenges. Domain-specific customization often requires substantial expertise in dataset curation and ethical considerations, such as preventing the propagation of biases inherent in industry-specific data. Addressing these issues

ensures that Falcon 40B remains a reliable tool across

specialized applications.

The Cohere Ecosystem: Streamlining Natural Language Applications

Cohere has positioned itself as a leader in accessible

AI, offering a comprehensive suite of tools that

simplify the development of natural language

applications. Its ecosystem is built around ease of use, providing APIs and pre-trained models that cater to a diverse range of developers, from startups to enterprise-level teams.

A key innovation in the Cohere ecosystem is its focus on semantic search and text generation. By optimizing its models for these tasks, Cohere enables businesses to implement intelligent search systems that retrieve relevant information based on context rather than keywords. This capability is particularly valuable in industries like e-commerce, where semantic search improves product discovery and customer satisfaction.

Another standout feature is Cohere's multilingual capabilities, which facilitate global applications without requiring extensive translation pipelines. By fine-tuning its models on a variety of languages and dialects, Cohere ensures that its tools are effective in culturally and linguistically diverse markets.

Cohere's deployment in chatbots and virtual assistants showcases its ability to handle complex conversational flows. By leveraging pre-trained conversational models, businesses can quickly deploy AI-driven systems that improve customer engagement and operational efficiency.

The future of the Cohere ecosystem lies in expanding its offerings to include domain-specific models and customizable APIs. This direction aligns with the growing demand for specialized tools that cater to unique business needs, from healthcare diagnostics to

legal research.

PaLM in the Enterprise: Unlocking Business Insights at Scale

PaLM's scalability and performance make it a natural fit for enterprise applications that demand robust data analysis and actionable insights. As a cornerstone of Google's AI offerings, PaLM has been integrated into tools that facilitate everything from workflow automation to strategic planning.

One of the most impactful applications of PaLM in the enterprise space is its role in knowledge management systems. By analyzing unstructured data from emails, documents, and meeting transcripts, PaLM can identify trends, highlight key information, and provide summaries that enhance decision-making processes.

In customer service, PaLM's conversational AI capabilities enable the creation of sophisticated virtual agents that can handle nuanced interactions. These agents not only resolve common queries but also escalate complex issues to human representatives with detailed context, improving both efficiency and customer satisfaction.

Marketing and sales teams leverage PaLM for personalized content generation, targeting specific audience segments with tailored messages. This capability is powered by PaLM's ability to analyze consumer behavior and predict preferences, ensuring campaigns are both effective and engaging.

PaLM's integration into enterprise applications highlights its versatility, but it also underscores the challenges of deploying such a powerful tool responsibly. Businesses must address concerns related to data privacy, model bias, and the potential for over-reliance on AI-driven decisions. By adopting transparent practices and robust monitoring systems, enterprises can mitigate these risks while maximizing the benefits of PaLM.

Beyond Text: Multimodal Capabilities in Bloom and the Future of AI

Bloom's multimodal extensions represent a leap forward in AI, demonstrating the potential of models that can process and generate data across multiple formats, including text, images, and audio. This capability paves the way for applications that demand a more holistic understanding of context and content.

The integration of multimodal capabilities into Bloom stems from advances in cross-attention mechanisms, which allow the model to correlate information across different modalities. For instance, when analyzing a dataset containing text and images, Bloom can identify relationships between textual descriptions and visual elements, enabling applications like automated video summarization and interactive storytelling.

In healthcare, Bloom's multimodal functionality is transformative. It can analyze medical images alongside patient records, assisting in diagnostics by correlating visual and textual data. Similarly, in education, Bloom enables the creation of interactive learning materials that combine text, visuals, and even audio explanations, catering to diverse learning styles.

Bloom's multimodal capabilities also extend to creative industries, where it powers tools for generating marketing content, designing virtual environments, and even composing music. By combining different forms of data, Bloom facilitates the creation of immersive experiences that push the boundaries of creativity.

Challenges in developing and deploying multimodal AI include ensuring data alignment across modalities and managing the increased computational complexity. However, as hardware accelerates and training techniques improve, multimodal systems like Bloom will play an increasingly central role in shaping the future of AI.

OpenAI Codex and the Revolution in Programming Assistance

OpenAI Codex has redefined the relationship between AI and software development, emerging as a revolutionary tool for programming assistance. By translating natural language into code, Codex simplifies the development process, making it accessible to non-programmers and increasing efficiency for experienced developers.

Codex's strength lies in its deep understanding of programming languages, frameworks, and libraries. Trained on a diverse dataset that includes public code repositories, it can generate code snippets, debug existing code, and even explain complex algorithms in plain language. This versatility is a game-changer for developers across industries.

In web development, Codex accelerates the creation of dynamic websites by generating boilerplate code and suggesting optimizations. Similarly, in data science, it aids in writing complex queries and scripts for data preprocessing, analysis, and visualization. Codex's ability to adapt to various programming languages ensures its utility in diverse technical domains.

Codex also plays a significant role in democratizing technology. By allowing users to describe desired functionalities in plain language, it bridges the gap between technical and non-technical stakeholders. This capability is particularly valuable in prototyping, where rapid iteration is essential for success.

Despite its strengths, Codex faces challenges, including the risk of generating insecure or inefficient code. To mitigate these issues, OpenAI has incorporated safety features and encourages users to review and test the code generated by the model. As Codex continues to evolve, its potential to revolutionize software development remains

unparalleled.

Exploring Vicuna: A New Paradigm for Lightweight

Large Language Models

Vicuna represents a significant shift toward

lightweight, efficient large language models designed

for resource-constrained environments. With a focus on achieving high performance at a lower computational cost, Vicuna has found its niche in applications where real-time processing and scalability are critical.

The architecture of Vicuna emphasizes parameter efficiency, leveraging innovations like low-rank adaptation (LoRA) and quantization techniques to reduce the model's memory footprint without sacrificing accuracy. This makes Vicuna an ideal candidate for edge deployments, such as mobile devices, IoT systems, and embedded AI applications.

In the automotive industry, Vicuna is employed in smart vehicles to provide natural language interfaces that process commands locally, ensuring fast response times while preserving user privacy. Similarly, in smart home systems, Vicuna powers voice assistants that operate seamlessly without relying on constant cloud connectivity.

Developers have also adopted Vicuna for real-time language translation in global events and remote collaboration platforms. Its ability to deliver accurate translations on low-power devices underscores its value in bridging language barriers without heavy infrastructure investments.

Despite its lightweight design, training and deploying Vicuna require careful balancing of trade-offs between speed and accuracy. Techniques such as sparsity optimization and knowledge distillation are integral to maintaining performance in constrained environments, making Vicuna a key player in the democratization of AI technology.

Falcon 40B and the Path to Ethical AI Deployment

Falcon 40B's success is not just a testament to its technical prowess but also a model for ethical AI deployment. As AI systems grow more powerful, ensuring they align with ethical principles becomes a priority, and Falcon 40B exemplifies how these principles can be implemented in practice.

One of the cornerstones of Falcon 40B's ethical framework is transparency. The model is designed to provide explanations for its outputs, enabling users to understand the reasoning behind its predictions or recommendations. This is particularly valuable in sensitive domains like healthcare and law, where accountability is paramount.

Bias mitigation is another area where Falcon 40B excels. By integrating diverse and representative training datasets, it minimizes the risk of perpetuating harmful stereotypes or inaccuracies. Additionally, regular audits and updates ensure the model remains fair and inclusive as societal norms evolve.

In education, Falcon 40B has been instrumental in creating personalized learning experiences while safeguarding student data privacy. Its deployment involves strict adherence to data protection regulations, demonstrating how ethical AI can coexist with innovative applications.

However, the ethical challenges Falcon 40B addresses are ongoing and dynamic. Developers and stakeholders must continuously engage with regulatory bodies, ethicists, and end-users to refine the model's implementation and ensure it remains a force for good in AI.

Collaborative AI Development: Bloom as a Case Study

Bloom stands as a beacon of collaborative AI development, showcasing how open-source initiatives can drive innovation while fostering inclusivity and shared ownership. Born from the collective efforts of researchers, developers, and organizations worldwide, Bloom represents a democratized approach to AI advancement.

Unlike proprietary models, Bloom was designed with transparency at its core, allowing researchers to explore its architecture, datasets, and training methods. This openness has spurred a wave of innovation, as developers build upon Bloom to create specialized models and tools tailored to diverse applications.

One notable application is in academia, where Bloom is used for research on language understanding, machine translation, and computational linguistics. Its open-source nature encourages collaboration among institutions, accelerating progress in these fields.

Bloom's influence extends to underrepresented languages and dialects. By providing an accessible platform for fine-tuning models on local datasets, Bloom empowers communities to preserve and promote linguistic diversity, addressing a gap often overlooked by commercial AI solutions.

The collaborative ethos of Bloom also raises questions about governance and accountability. As more contributors join the ecosystem, ensuring quality, security, and ethical alignment becomes a shared responsibility. Bloom's governance framework, which emphasizes community-driven decision-making, offers a blueprint for navigating these complexities.

PaLM's Contribution to Creative AI: Beyond Automation

PaLM has emerged as a powerful tool for creative industries, transcending its role as an automation engine to become a collaborator in art, literature, and design. Its ability to generate text, images, and other media positions it as a versatile asset in creative workflows.

In publishing, PaLM assists authors by generating plot ideas, character arcs, and even entire chapters. While it doesn't replace human creativity, its suggestions often spark new directions and overcome writer's block. Similarly, in the gaming industry, PaLM contributes to world-building by generating detailed narratives, dialogues, and immersive lore.

The fashion industry leverages PaLM for trend analysis and design inspiration. By analyzing social media, historical trends, and consumer preferences, the model identifies emerging patterns and suggests innovative design elements. PaLM's generative capabilities are also employed in creating promotional content, such as slogans and advertisements, tailored to specific audiences.

However, PaLM's integration into creative processes is not without challenges. Ethical questions about authorship, originality, and compensation arise when

AI contributes significantly to a creative work. Establishing guidelines for attribution and collaboration ensures that human and AI creators coexist harmoniously.

PaLM's role in creative industries exemplifies how AI can augment, rather than replace, human ingenuity, opening new frontiers in collaborative creation.

Scaling LLM Deployment: Lessons from Cohere

Deploying large language models (LLMs) at scale is a complex undertaking, requiring careful planning and execution to balance performance, cost, and accessibility. Cohere's journey in scaling its models offers valuable lessons for organizations navigating similar challenges.

One of Cohere's key innovations is its deployment of federated learning, which enables model training across distributed datasets without compromising data privacy. This approach has been pivotal in industries like finance and healthcare, where sensitive data must remain secure while benefiting from AI advancements.

Cohere also emphasizes infrastructure optimization. By leveraging cloud-native technologies and serverless architectures, it reduces the operational burden of maintaining high-performance AI systems. These optimizations allow Cohere to deliver real-time applications, such as chatbots and search engines, at a global scale.

Another critical factor in Cohere's scalability is its commitment to user-centric design. By offering customizable APIs and developer-friendly tools, it empowers businesses to integrate LLMs seamlessly into their existing workflows. This accessibility drives adoption across a wide range of industries, from retail to legal services.

The challenges of scaling LLMs, such as latency, cost management, and model retraining, are addressed through continuous monitoring and iterative improvements. Cohere's focus on sustainable scaling demonstrates that operational excellence and cutting-edge AI can coexist, setting a benchmark for the industry.

Part III: The Future of LLM Technologies

This section explores the broader landscape of LLM

development and its potential impact on the future.

Chapter 8: Emerging Trends in LLM Development

The field of LLMs is constantly evolving, with exciting

trends shaping the future:

- **Focus on interpretability and explainability:** As LLMs become more complex, ensuring we understand how they arrive at their outputs is crucial. Research is ongoing to make LLMs more transparent, allowing us to identify and address potential biases.

- **Multimodal learning:** Going beyond text, LLMs are being developed to incorporate information from images, code, and other formats. This will enable them to understand the world in a more holistic way.

- **Smaller, more efficient models:** While massive models have dominated the field, there's a push for creating effective LLMs with fewer parameters. This would make them more accessible and less computationally expensive.

- **Focus on real-world applications:** The research community is increasingly focused on developing LLMs that can solve real-world problems. We can expect advancements in areas like healthcare, education, and customer service.

Chapter 9: Ethical Considerations and Responsible AI Practices

As LLMs become more powerful, ethical

considerations become paramount:

- **Bias and fairness:** LLMs inherit biases from the

  data they are trained on. It's crucial to develop

methods to mitigate bias and ensure fair treatment for everyone.

- **Transparency and explainability:** As mentioned earlier, understanding how LLMs arrive at their outputs is essential for building trust and addressing potential issues.

- **Accountability and safety:** It's important to establish clear guidelines and frameworks for the development and deployment of LLMs to ensure responsible use and mitigate potential risks.

Case Study: Bloom in Preserving Indigenous Languages

Bloom has been instrumental in addressing the digital divide for indigenous languages, providing a platform for linguistic preservation and revitalization. In one project in South America, Bloom was used to develop resources for an endangered Amazonian language spoken by fewer than 10,000 people.

Linguists and local community leaders collaborated to create a dataset of oral histories, traditional songs, and cultural narratives. Bloom was fine-tuned on this dataset to generate teaching materials, including digital flashcards, grammar guides, and practice exercises. The resulting tools were implemented in local schools and community centers, fostering intergenerational learning.

Despite its success, challenges such as data scarcity and cultural sensitivities were significant. The team ensured ethical considerations were at the forefront, securing informed consent and employing native speakers as annotators to maintain authenticity. The project's success has inspired similar initiatives globally, showcasing Bloom's versatility in preserving cultural heritage.

Case Study: Vicuna in Smart Home Devices

Vicuna has become a preferred choice for smart home devices, particularly in regions with limited internet access. A startup in rural Africa utilized Vicuna to develop a low-cost, offline smart home assistant capable of controlling appliances, answering queries, and providing weather updates.

The compact architecture of Vicuna allowed the system to run efficiently on low-power devices, such as Raspberry Pi boards. The assistant was pre-trained on datasets relevant to the local language and cultural context, ensuring accurate and relatable responses.

The deployment faced challenges, such as adapting to various dialects and maintaining energy efficiency.

Regular updates and community feedback were key to overcoming these hurdles. The project demonstrated how Vicuna could bridge the gap between advanced AI technologies and underserved communities.

Case Study: PaLM in Automated Scriptwriting

A leading film studio integrated PaLM into its pre-production process to streamline scriptwriting. PaLM was tasked with generating draft scripts based on genre-specific prompts and plot outlines, significantly reducing the time required to create initial drafts.

Writers used PaLM's outputs as a starting point, refining plots, dialogues, and character arcs. This collaborative approach allowed them to focus more on creativity rather than repetitive tasks. For example, a sci-fi series benefited from PaLM's ability to create complex, interconnected subplots, providing depth to the narrative.

Ethical considerations, such as authorship and intellectual property rights, were carefully addressed. Writers retained creative control, and AI-generated contributions were transparently documented. The integration of PaLM highlighted the potential of AI in augmenting human creativity without replacing it.

Case Study: Cohere in E-commerce Personalization

Cohere was adopted by a global e-commerce platform to enhance customer experience through personalized recommendations. Using its advanced natural language understanding capabilities, Cohere analyzed user queries, browsing histories, and purchase patterns to deliver tailored product suggestions in real-time.

The platform also deployed Cohere for dynamic search improvements. For instance, ambiguous queries like "comfortable shoes" were resolved contextually, presenting options that matched the user's preferences.

Challenges included managing computational costs and ensuring data privacy. Cohere's federated learning framework helped address these issues, enabling model updates without compromising user data. The implementation resulted in a 30% increase in customer engagement and a significant boost in sales, proving Cohere's effectiveness in large-scale deployments.

Case Study: Falcon 40B in Healthcare Chatbots

A hospital network in Europe deployed Falcon 40B to power a patient-facing chatbot for appointment scheduling, symptom checking, and health advice. The model's advanced language comprehension enabled it to handle complex medical queries with precision.

Trained on anonymized patient data and medical literature, Falcon 40B provided accurate, context-aware responses. Its explainability feature allowed patients to understand the reasoning behind recommendations, building trust in the system.

The project faced hurdles, such as regulatory compliance and ensuring unbiased advice. Regular audits and updates ensured adherence to ethical guidelines. The chatbot reduced administrative burdens, allowing medical staff to focus on patient care, and demonstrated how AI could enhance healthcare accessibility.

Case Study: Bloom in Legal Document Analysis

A multinational law firm adopted Bloom to streamline the analysis of legal documents, contracts, and case law. The model was fine-tuned to identify key clauses, flag potential risks, and summarize lengthy texts, saving hours of manual work.

Bloom's ability to process multilingual data was particularly useful for cross-border cases. It translated and contextualized legal terms, enabling seamless collaboration among international teams.

Challenges included ensuring data confidentiality and adapting the model to niche legal jargon. By implementing robust encryption and customizing training data, the firm successfully mitigated these issues. The adoption of Bloom demonstrated its potential to revolutionize the legal industry by enhancing efficiency and accuracy.

Case Study: Vicuna in Disaster Response Systems

Vicuna was used to develop an AI-driven disaster response system in Southeast Asia, focusing on real-time communication and resource allocation during emergencies. The model powered multilingual chat interfaces for affected populations to report incidents and request aid.

Vicuna's lightweight design enabled deployment on portable devices, ensuring connectivity in remote or disaster-stricken areas. Its real-time capabilities helped responders prioritize actions and distribute resources effectively.

Challenges included handling high traffic volumes and ensuring message clarity across languages. Advanced optimization techniques and continuous testing ensured the system's reliability. The project showcased how Vicuna could play a crucial role in saving lives during crises.

Case Study: PaLM in Educational Technology

An EdTech company integrated PaLM into its platform to create adaptive learning modules for students. The model analyzed individual performance data to tailor quizzes, tutorials, and feedback, fostering a personalized learning experience.

PaLM's multilingual capabilities allowed the platform to cater to diverse student populations. For instance, math problems were contextualized using culturally relevant examples, making learning more engaging and relatable.

Implementation challenges included managing the vast data generated and ensuring equity in recommendations. The company addressed these issues through robust data pipelines and regular audits. PaLM's integration demonstrated the transformative potential of AI in education, making it more inclusive and effective.

Case Study: Falcon 40B in Content Moderation

A social media platform employed Falcon 40B to enhance content moderation, focusing on detecting harmful speech, misinformation, and policy violations. The model was fine-tuned on diverse datasets to improve its understanding of nuanced language and cultural contexts.

Falcon 40B's real-time processing capabilities enabled moderators to respond quickly to flagged content, reducing the spread of harmful material. Its explainability features also helped users understand moderation decisions, improving transparency and trust.

The project faced challenges such as balancing freedom of expression with community safety. Continuous monitoring and iterative updates ensured the system remained fair and effective. Falcon 40B's role in content moderation highlighted its potential to create safer online environments.

Case Study: Cohere in Financial Document Processing

A global investment firm implemented Cohere to automate the analysis of financial reports and market trends. The model processed large volumes of unstructured data, extracting key insights and generating summaries for decision-makers.

Cohere's ability to understand complex financial terminology and generate actionable recommendations significantly reduced the time spent on manual analysis. For instance, it flagged discrepancies in quarterly reports and identified emerging market opportunities.

Data security and model interpretability were critical challenges. By employing robust encryption and explainable AI techniques, the firm ensured compliance with industry regulations. Cohere's deployment illustrated the potential of LLMs in transforming financial operations through enhanced efficiency and accuracy.

Chapter 10: The Future Impact of LLMs on Society

LLMs have the potential to revolutionize various aspects of society:

- **Enhanced automation:** LLMs can automate many tasks currently performed by humans, increasing efficiency in various sectors.

- **Personalized experiences:** LLMs can personalize experiences in areas like education, healthcare, and entertainment by tailoring content and recommendations to individual needs.

- **Improved communication and collaboration:** LLMs can break down language barriers and facilitate communication across cultures. They can also assist with collaborative tasks by summarizing information or generating different creative text formats to brainstorm ideas.

- **New forms of creativity:** LLMs can inspire and assist with creative endeavors, acting as co-

creators or generating new ideas and
possibilities.

However, it's important to acknowledge potential
challenges:

- **Job displacement:** Automation through LLMs
  could lead to job displacement in certain sectors.
  It's crucial to focus on retraining and reskilling
  initiatives.

- **Misinformation and bias:** If not carefully
  addressed, LLMs could exacerbate the spread of
  misinformation and perpetuate existing biases.

- **The digital divide:** Unequal access to LLM
  technologies could create a digital divide,
  further marginalizing certain communities.

Harnessing Cohere for Scalable Multilingual Applications

Cohere has proven to be a robust solution for organizations requiring multilingual support at scale. A global customer service platform integrated Cohere to enhance its language capabilities, enabling seamless communication across diverse regions. With its ability to understand and generate responses in over 100 languages, the model became a cornerstone of the platform's success.

One of Cohere's standout applications involved real-time translation for customer queries. By fine-tuning the model with industry-specific terminology and customer feedback, the platform ensured accurate and context-aware translations. This allowed agents to handle queries in languages they did not speak natively, bridging linguistic gaps and improving overall customer satisfaction.

The platform also utilized Cohere for sentiment analysis in various languages, enabling it to prioritize urgent or negative feedback. By integrating these insights into its workflow, the organization reduced resolution times and improved customer retention.

However, scaling multilingual applications presented unique challenges. Regional dialects, idiomatic expressions, and cultural nuances often led to misunderstandings. To address this, the platform adopted a cyclical fine-tuning approach, where user interactions continuously informed model updates. Moreover, privacy concerns were managed by employing federated learning and end-to-end encryption, ensuring data remained secure.

The scalability of Cohere demonstrated its potential to transcend traditional linguistic barriers. By integrating with real-time systems and leveraging cloud-based deployment, the platform expanded its reach while maintaining low latency. The project underscored the model's capacity for broad, impactful use in global customer service.

Advanced Applications of Falcon 40B in Autonomous Systems

Falcon 40B has emerged as a leader in autonomous systems, enabling significant advancements in robotics, drones, and self-driving vehicles. Its ability to process large-scale data streams in real-time has made it indispensable for decision-making and operational efficiency.

One compelling use case involved Falcon 40B in autonomous drone fleets for disaster management. These drones, equipped with sensors and cameras, transmitted real-time data to the model, which analyzed terrain, weather, and resource requirements. Falcon 40B's contextual understanding enabled the drones to prioritize rescue operations, deliver medical supplies, and assess damage with minimal human intervention.

In the automotive sector, Falcon 40B was integrated into self-driving systems to enhance situational awareness. By processing inputs from LiDAR, cameras, and GPS, the model predicted potential hazards and optimized driving routes. Unlike traditional algorithms, Falcon 40B exhibited superior adaptability, handling complex scenarios such as crowded intersections or adverse weather conditions.

The implementation of Falcon 40B in autonomous systems required overcoming several technical challenges. Computational efficiency was critical for real-time processing, which led to the adoption of edge computing techniques. Additionally, safety concerns necessitated rigorous testing and fail-safe mechanisms. Engineers conducted extensive simulations and real-world trials to validate the model's performance under diverse conditions.

Another challenge involved ensuring ethical and legal compliance, particularly in scenarios with potential risks to human lives. Transparency in decision-making was addressed through Falcon 40B's explainability features, which provided clear reasoning behind its actions.

The deployment of Falcon 40B in autonomous systems represents a significant leap in AI-driven technologies. Its ability to learn and adapt to dynamic

environments has paved the way for safer, more

efficient autonomous solutions, demonstrating the

transformative potential of LLMs in real-world

applications.

Revolutionizing Healthcare Diagnostics with PaLM

PaLM (Pathways Language Model) has been pivotal in transforming healthcare diagnostics by enhancing speed and accuracy in clinical decision-making. A prominent use case involved its deployment in radiology for analyzing medical imaging, such as X-rays, MRIs, and CT scans.

The model was fine-tuned using extensive datasets of annotated medical images, enabling it to detect anomalies with remarkable precision. In a pilot study conducted at a leading hospital, PaLM identified early signs of lung cancer in X-rays with an accuracy rate of over 95%, outperforming conventional diagnostic methods. Radiologists used PaLM-generated insights as a secondary validation layer, which reduced diagnostic errors and expedited treatment plans.

Beyond imaging, PaLM played a critical role in electronic health record (EHR) analysis. By parsing complex medical histories, the model identified patterns and correlations that human clinicians might overlook. For example, it flagged potential drug interactions and suggested alternative therapies based on patient profiles.

The integration of PaLM into healthcare systems posed challenges, such as ensuring compliance with stringent regulations like HIPAA and GDPR. To address these, the development team implemented robust data anonymization protocols and secure on-premises deployment. Ethical concerns, such as algorithmic bias, were mitigated through continuous model retraining on diverse datasets to ensure equitable outcomes across demographics.

One groundbreaking application was in telemedicine, where PaLM powered virtual assistants for remote consultations. Patients could describe symptoms in natural language, and the model provided preliminary diagnoses and recommendations, enhancing access to healthcare in underserved areas.

PaLM's contributions to healthcare diagnostics demonstrate the profound impact of LLMs in life-critical domains. By augmenting human expertise with AI-driven insights, the model has set a new standard for efficiency and accuracy in medical practice.

Empowering Creative Industries with Bloom

Bloom has emerged as a creative powerhouse, revolutionizing industries like advertising, content creation, and game development. Its ability to generate high-quality, contextually relevant text has opened new possibilities for creative professionals.

One notable application involved a global advertising agency using Bloom to craft personalized marketing campaigns. By analyzing customer data and preferences, Bloom generated compelling ad copy tailored to specific audiences. For instance, in a campaign for a fitness brand, the model created dynamic slogans and narratives that resonated with diverse demographics, increasing engagement by 40%.

In the gaming industry, Bloom was utilized to design intricate storylines and character dialogues for role-playing games (RPGs). Developers provided initial plot outlines, and the model expanded them into rich, immersive narratives. Players praised the natural flow of dialogues and the depth of character development, attributing it to Bloom's creative capabilities.

Challenges in creative applications included maintaining originality and avoiding plagiarism.

Developers ensured Bloom's outputs were unique by incorporating extensive datasets while excluding copyrighted material. Additionally, iterative feedback loops with human creators refined the model's outputs, striking a balance between AI automation and human creativity.

Another innovative use case was in publishing, where Bloom assisted authors in generating ideas, drafting chapters, and editing manuscripts. In one project, a science fiction author collaborated with Bloom to brainstorm futuristic technologies and plot twists, resulting in a best-selling novel.

Bloom also demonstrated potential in multimedia content creation by generating scripts for short films and commercials. Its ability to adapt to various genres and tones made it a versatile tool for creative professionals.

By streamlining workflows and enhancing creative output, Bloom has empowered industries to achieve unprecedented levels of productivity and innovation. Its role in shaping the future of creative work highlights the transformative potential of AI in fostering human ingenuity.

Conclusion

The development of LLMs is an ongoing journey with immense potential to benefit society. By prioritizing responsible development, ethical considerations, and a focus on real-world applications, LLMs can become powerful tools for progress. As we move forward, it's crucial to ensure this technology serves humanity and helps us build a better future.

www.ingramcontent.com/pod-product-compliance
Lightning Source LLC
LaVergne TN
LVHW051702050326
832903LV00032B/3954